History of a Woman

History of a Woman

Laura A. Lord

History of a Woman

"Time for Church" was previously published in *The Collegian.*

ISBN-13: 978-1480251854

Art: © Ipb | Dreamstime.com

Second Printing

To the Man…Yeah, you're cool and all. But seriously, I love you…with all I am and all I hope to be. You make me a better person.

And to my brother: your Republican ways to my Liberal Plans, your ego to my feminist, your stubbornness to my, well, stubbornness. I love you through it all.

Special Thanks to my editor, Gloria Condrell.

And to Linda Earls, Dave Harper, Liz O'Connor, Juliet Smith, and Ed Baker: thank you for pushing me, molding me, and supporting me along the way.

Out of the ash

I rise with my red hair

And I eat men like air.

- **Sylvia Plath, *Lady Lazarus***

History is her story.

History of a Woman

Laura A. Lord

Table of Contents

History of a Woman

History of a Woman

The girls made their way down the winding dirt road, their white dresses flapping gently against their bony knees. They were linked, hand-in-hand, fingers entwined, feet moving in the same rhythm. Two girls became one, melded and meshed until anyone looking saw one set of dark eyes, one little, white dress, one pair of bobby socks and tennis shoes.

So they said, "I need something. Something to make me shine. I look like every other girl. I need to find my fire."

And as one they reached out. They grabbed the electric fence on the side of that dirt road, that border between cow and field, between man and earth, between "we" and "I".

The current shot through them. It made a wide loop through their chest, pumped through their fast-beating heart, coiled in their stomach and shot out of their fingertips with the carefully trimmed and clean nails. It lit up the world and the girls shone bright as a beacon, as the star over Bethlehem, as a lighthouse on a rocky shore, as the perfect edges of a solar eclipse.

Down the road came the old women. Their wrinkled skin and crooked limbs illuminated by the girls. They wore faces carved by worry, haste, and disgust. They wore old housecoats and nightgowns. They wore hats and scarves to cover their hair. They were empty of any embellishment, extravagant in their very own settled ways.

"You'll bring the men!" They yelled at the girls, panic evident in their voices. "You aren't ready."

So the old women gathered. They lifted their skirts and pulled free baskets of laundry, tubs of hot water, dirty dishes, pants and irons, rags and sponges, sides of beef and potatoes with the peels still intact. They lifted their skirts and pulled out the tools of their trade and said, "Learn. What will you do when he asks for the beat biscuits to be made like his mother did?"

But the girls' hands were full of fence and light. So they opened their chest and new arms came out. New hands grew and fumbled around. They took up the laundry, the beef, and the pants. They sewed buttons, washed forks, and punched the dough into the bowl.

When they'd finished, the road beneath them was paved. The black tar radiated heat that made the old women fan themselves as they walked off, mumbling.

"Did it well enough, I suppose."

"Did you see the crease in those pants?"

"Shameful."

The girl's hands stayed full, working past exhaustion. Their light still bright and drawing the young women, who in short day dresses, in pencil skirts and high-heeled shoes, in bangle bracelets and pearl studs, in short trench coats and free-flowing hair came running down the road.

"Stop!" They yelled at the girls. "You'll bring the men. I've seen them. They're coming!"

So the young women gathered around the girls and lifted their skirts. They reached up and pulled out books and paper, maps and pens, musical instruments and sets of oil pastels. They pulled out the new tools and said, "Learn. What will you do when he asks the longitude of Memphis?"

But the girls' hands were full and they couldn't let go of the fence for fear of losing their precious light. So they opened their chest again and more arms sprang free. The hands grabbed at the pages, flipping, turning, devouring every little phrase.

Around them the cows went away. The fields disappeared and a development of postcard picture houses popped up. Picket fences marked the boundaries and basketball hoops stood like sentries at the foot of every driveway. The young women left them, flipping their loose hair.

"Couldn't even find Albuquerque."

"Not a single original thought."

"They tried. They tried."

And so the girls were left with the pressed pants and the peeled potatoes, with the maps of colonies and the stars and stripes, with cups and saucers full of the total percent of the third greatest export of Cyprus.

But the men had seen the light and in their casual time, their easy manner, they passed the old women who dipped their heads to stare at their feet. They passed the young women who stepped back out of the way. They found the girls and dropped their pants. They stood there, flaccid cocks against their thighs and said, "Please me."

Again the girls tried to open their chest, but there was no more room. No room for more arms, more hands and fingers. So the men put their hands on the girls' shoulders and pushed them to their knees. And the girls changed the current. They opened their mouth and gave their fire away. They swallowed the men and made them shine.

Laura A. Lord

How Bad Is It

That I don't remember
how we met,
or where I found you,
or even if it was me?
Who did the finding,
or the being found,
or was even lost,
to begin with?
You asked me to shave
my legs in front of the
camera. Guess you needed
a bit of normal in the
midst of your war.
I'm a firm believer in the
necessity of estrogen
and implementing it
through a thin sheen of glass
with a hazy video feed
playing and playing and
playing. You would stand,
slowly, before the camera
to showcase the flat expanse
of your stomach. To think for
a moment, I didn't believe you were
interested. Silly me.
Silly girl.
Silly woman.
Silly romantic song you sang me
and handed over like a newspaper

and duct tape wrapped gift.
Something to cherish, 'cause
with all that wrapping
there was no way in hell
I'd ever get it open.
I'd lay my hand on the screen
and the digital pixels
and vast distance
distorted our shape,
our size, until for a moment
it looked as if they were the same.
You asked me to come to
California
and in the same breath
told me about your wife.
How lovely.
An entire country away
and all I wanted to do
was sit at my desk
with a tin bowl of hot water,
a razor blade in my grasp.

Woman's Jive Tune

My up and down
Are left and right
And topsy-turvy's
On my breakfast plate
Upside down is every day
I climb out from under my
"Hey, I'm okay"
And the life blood drips
To coffee brown stains
In the shape of Africa
On kitchen counters
Cabinets
Refrigerators
And ovens
And a fancy new microwave
That cooks everything on
Cremate
So it's, "Cinderella, Cinderella,"
While I'm mopping up the dishes
While I'm folding all the dust bunnies
And tucking them in closets
And it's "Cinderella, Cinderella"
While I'm scrubbing at the noises
While I'm vacuuming the pain away
And dancing to the tune
Of the garbage disposal gurgle
Blug blug blug
To the tune of the garbage disposal gurgle
I'm Cinderella

In a house full of midgets
Peons
Insignifi-cunts
And oh, do we love a visitor
The dining table's huge
We could feed a small army
On misconceptions
On grief and heartache
On every day abuse
We could fill their bellies
On lies and mistrust
On fables and myths
Of a family in love
And we could steal their souls
As we pass the gravy boat
Keep them trapped in here with us
Where there's no up or down
Or right or left
"And pass the crazy, please…
It's over there on the box where she keeps the…"
Please make it go
Away

Time for Church

"Please, just get up Garrett." Her fingers twitched at the corner of the blanket, yanking it back from over his face in one swift move. "I have to get ready," Lauren complained, practically pleading with him to get out of the bed. Their room was hot already, the summer morning air thick and heavy as it lingered in the attic bedroom. Even with the windows open, no breeze came through to stir the little dust motes through the sunrays that blasted their way into the room through large, curtain-less windows. Sweat had been mingling on her skin all morning, but after her fifth time up the stairs it had started to bead and glue her hair to the sides of her face and neck.

Garrett rolled onto his side, opening one dull, blue eye to glare at her. "I went on a call last night, woman. Let me sleep." Lauren knew she had assumed her mother's stance: the hands on her hips, the right leg pushed out just a bit further than the other, and her teeth gritted together. "I have church in twenty minutes. Just come downstairs and watch the girls so I can get in the shower."

He grumbled some response that sounded nothing like a "yes", but even so, his short, stocky frame slid out from under the covers and his heavy footsteps pounded down the staircase. Lauren followed behind him a few moments later, a green, sleeveless, summer dress in her arms and a pair of white heels fighting for purchase in fingers that clung to the straps along with a thin silver chain and a pair of small hooped earrings.

Downstairs she found him, sprawled on the couch with the Xbox controller in his hand, while the girls sat in from of the TV in their Easter dresses, a sprawl of dolls and ponies in their laps. "I'll be right back out," she called as she made her way through the living room and into the bathroom, passing her son who was sleeping in his car seat by the living room entrance.

The water was never hot, but she managed after enough twisting of the loose knob to get it at least lukewarm. Still in a rush, she had her clothes off and in a pile on the thread bare bathmat in no time. Lauren slipped in and let the water beat off her skin, wiping away the morning's sweat and grime. One, two…four splinters littered her middle finger. Putting the digit between her teeth, she pulled them out and spit them down the drain.

She was the queen of multitasking and as she had shampoo in her hair, she was scrubbing her body down with the bar of soap. When all that had been rinsed, she added conditioner, washed her face clean and let the water wash away the last of the bubbles. It was just as the water was spitting more cold than warm that she shut it off, flipped her long, black locks over and shook her wet hair out. The red bath towel, her favorite, was large enough to wrap around her entire body, though after only a few minutes out of the shower she had to open the door to let the steam out.

Her body was already sticky with sweat and for the thousandth time she sent a silent prayer up for an air conditioner. *Just drop one out of the air. I really don't give a shit where it comes from; just give me some cold air.* Her bare feet left small puddles on the floor as she

made her way back out into the living room to find
Garrett sound asleep on the couch.

A quick look down showed her son, still asleep,
but hot enough that his thin, baby hair had clung in wet
lumps to his head. Lauren reached down and ruffled it
softly, earning a soft sigh from him as he rolled his head
against her fingers. A little half smile crept across her
lips, before she heard the Family Guy theme song. "You
guys can't watch...," her voice broke off as she realized
the girls weren't sitting there in front of the TV. Lauren
looked down at the pile of toys on the floor and then
moved down to the hall to push the girls' bedroom door
open.

"Hailey? Daphne?" Her voice was loud enough
that they should have heard her, but two year olds were
hardly reliable to answer right away.

"No hiding guys. C'mon out," Lauren called,
popping further down the hall to look in her son's room.
Not there either. Her fingers flexed around the towel,
tucking it in further to keep it from falling down her
body. Back in the living room Garrett continued to snore
away and it was when Lauren moved to wake him that
she saw it. The front door was open.

Not such a big deal this far back in the country. It
wasn't as if their house sat right on the highway. In fact,
only corn fields surrounded their little half acre of land.
They know better, Lauren thought. The girls wouldn't
have gone outside by themselves. When she moved to
close the front door she saw a flash of yellow.

Two pale yellow dresses flapped in the breeze,
the green and pink flowers on them fuzzed out of detail
by the distance. Two pale little hands grasped one

another, brown hair floating behind them in matching ponytails. Part of the field had been cut already and the combine was turning for another circle.

Without a sound, Lauren dashed out the door and ran barefooted across the field. The girls were almost to the corn, the combine headed right for them. *He doesn't see them.* Her landlord, the old man who owned the farm next door was sitting up in the combine. He waved a hand to Lauren as she raced, waving her arms at him. Yet still, he pushed on, as if to meet her halfway with the big machine.

The sharp spikes of corn husks bit into her feet, tearing the soft skin of her soles. Her feet sunk into the dirt, catching her and tripping her as she struggled to make it to the girls. Even still the sputter of the machine roared around her, drowning out her screams and vibrating the very ground she ran on. Ten more feet, maybe, the girls would be in the corn. The golden stalks rose even above Lauren's head. She'd never find them in there.

The towel had fallen from her body somewhere along her run, leaving her naked skin open to the sun and making the sweat glisten on her. Her breath hitched and a pain stabbed through her side, her lungs struggling to keep up the pace her terrified body had set. Two more feet and she grabbed them, sweeping both girls into her arms and crushing them against her chest. Tears were running and falling down onto the top of their heads as Lauren sat there in the dirt sobbing in relief.

The motor shut off and by the time her landlord had made his way over to the trio all three were crying, Lauren in fear and regret, the girls simply because their mother was crying. "We wanna ride the tractor," a small voice whispered, the soft breath falling on her neck and Lauren sobbed louder, clenching them tight against her. "No. No, not again. Don't—Don't do it again. No. Please, no."

"Where's your clothes, girl?" Lauren looked up to see her landlord, red-faced in embarrassment and kicking at the dirt with his shoes. He looked almost angry with her, as if he was offended that she was running around his field without a stitch to cover herself. "My girls…," she started, but he rudely cut her off. "Just get home and get some clothes on. Bad example for those girls." He muttered something about her being late for church before going back to his combine.

The motor rumbled to life and Lauren flinched, waiting until she saw it turn and head back towards the barns in the distance before she stood, taking a girl in each arm and carrying them back to the house. They were late for church and she needed a shower.

Back, Back, Back

They were celebrating their 58th wedding anniversary.
Children, grandchildren, great grandchildren, people
they weren't even related to, filled the room at the fire
hall. The noise was a hum, a vibration, which swept
through her old bones and made her teeth rattle. She
watched her husband walk across the room, from one
end to another. She watched him shake hands with
everyone who spoke to him. He looked, when she
focused on him, like a younger version of himself. A
smile crossed her lips as she saw him grasp a woman's
hands with both of his. He leaned forward and kissed her
on the cheek, standing back to look into the face of the
woman he'd been having an affair with for over fifteen
years.

*****

She bent over the table, holding a hand over the top
of her dress to keep the cloth from dipping down into the
gravy boat as she held the long match to the candles in
the center. Once all three were lit, she blew the match
out, trailing a puff of grey smoke behind her. Flicking
the switch on the wall, the lights went out and only the
dim glow of the candles lit up the table. It was laden
down with plates and bowls, full of his favorite meal. An
hour later, the woman was checking her reflection in the
back of a spoon, setting it back down beside her empty
plate, and adjusting it so it lay nicely next to the knife.
Two hours later, she called his cell phone, only to get his
voicemail. Again. Three hours later, she was on the
phone with his office where, according to the sweet-

sounding, twenty-something woman on the line, there had been no meeting called for today . Four hours later, the woman blew out the candles, scooped up a piece of meat and covered it in congealing gravy. She ate.

*****

He'd been arrested and she'd been released. "Can't stay here," they said. So she wandered across town. She held her arms tight around her chest, hugging the humid air into her space. The third church of the evening held a door that wasn't locked. And she snuck through the kitchen and up a set of stairs. She passed the metal chairs and raided a closet of choir gowns. Bunching them up into something resembling a pillow, she laid down on the hard, wooden floor. She counted the minutes until morning. The minutes until his release, her reunion. For the first time in years she prayed. She prayed time would stop.

The Check

The check came once a week and on it, in the tiny, informal script she could see the statistics. She saw the demographics, the signatures, the dates, the times, the dollar signs and the cents. The sense. Pay to the order of the single mother, the broken hearted, the lost and struggling. Pay to the order of that bitch who walked out, that gold-digger, that useless leech.

Twenty dollars and thirty-two cents. Thirty-six dollars and seventeen cents. That was the breakdown. That was division at work. That was the price tag, per child, per absent father, per paycheck, as ordered by the court.

So her son was worth $20.32 a week. He was worth one pair of sneakers, plus tax. He was worth a family dinner from KFC. He was worth two Wal-Mart brand t-shirts and a pair of jeans with the little buttons inside to adjust the waist so they wouldn't fall off his thin hips. He was worth one pack of the good brand of nighttime pull-ups and a fruity flavored Tummy Yummy.

$36.17. She was worth fifteen dollars and eighty-five cents more than her brother. And why was that? Because she is the older of the two? Because she came first? Because she was left behind first? That extra fifteen dollars and eighty-five cents makes her worth ice-cream at school for an entire month. She is worth two of those scarves from Target that she wants, because all the other little girls are wearing them. Thirty-six seventeen means she is worth one new dress and stockings to match. She's worth a movie date with her mom and maybe, just maybe, she's worth popcorn with extra butter.

She stares at the names and the dates and the amounts. She pulls out her calculator, because she's logical, because she's sane, because she knows there must be some algorithm in play that dictates the price attached to another human being's name, date of birth, and social security number. Somewhere inside her children's DNA is the bar code that is engraved with all this information. That's why she couldn't find it. That's why the numbers never came out right.

One month is $81.28 and $144.68. That's school supplies for both, new book-bags and lunch boxes, and for her daughter, that means she's worth a new pair of dress shoes where her toes won't hang over the edge.

One year makes them worth $975.36 and $1736.16. He is four, so that means he's worth $3901.44. She's six, so it's $10,416.96. Right? That makes sense, she figured. I mean, by the time they are grown, their price-tag will be immense. They will be worth so much...so very, very much.

And that was the game. It was all a gamble. They had set the bet and she had called. Not only had she called, but she'd raised. She's raised and raised and raised. She met each of their bets and double and tripled them. She'd paid in her part, and not only with money, but with her time. With her kisses, her late night wake-up calls, her trips to the family doctor, her white hairs, her once a month new toothbrushes, her story times.

So when those men would show back up, she'd be able to look them in the eye. She'd be able to say,

"Hey, I figured it out." She knew her child's worth and she'd raised the bet. "It's on you now. Call or fold."

Heredity of Peas

"You better get it through your head now, girl," Elaine began, breaking her silence as the long, slim end of ash from her cigarette hung dangerously off the tip. "Ain't nothin' from a man goin' to be any good for you. Nothin'." She tapped the cigarette on the edge of the clear, crystal tray, sending the scraps of dust climbing up the sides. "What you get from them anyway? Hmm? Bag o' split peas?" Elaine motioned with one crooked, arthritis-choked finger to the bag I held to my face.

The frozen peas, the plastic bag, slipped in my hands and rubbed the tiny beads against the soft surface of my cheek. I'd lost all feeling to my eye, frozen the tear ducts and finally shut them off. I looked at her across the table, sitting there in her old, flannel housedress, a faded, blue bandana wrapped around the wispy white hair that poked up and out in all directions. Smoke billowed around Elaine as if she were on fire, constantly on fire. I focused on those floating circles and swirls, watching them light up in the rays of sun from the window over the sink. I watched the particles of dust mixing, mating, and separating again within those rays.

Elaine continued as if I hadn't ignored her question, as if I'd answered her just how she wanted. "Bag o' peas. That's what you got. Some peas and menstrual cycles and menopause and a hysterectomy and meningitis and history. You got history. You got God made the world and He saw it was good. He saw it. You see?"

"Act like I haven't heard those lines in Sunday school every morning. Like I don't know those verses," I said, blunt and blatant and bumbling like a child.

"'Course you heard them, but you ain't been listenin'. You got to listen to it, to hear it." Elaine paused, sucking deeply off her menthol cigarette, smoke floating out of her nostrils like the angry bull from the *Bug's Bunny* cartoons. "You got the Father and the Son and the Holy Ghost…a whole, holy trinity o' men. You got the world He made and He said it was good. We didn't say it. He said it. Not like we goin' to argue with Him none. Nope, He said it, so it's got to be."

I moved the peas down from my face, squinting out of my swollen eye and setting the dripping bag onto the table top. "The whole world's not bad…" I began, quickly cut off by her hacking laughter, her smoker's cough, her insolence and her life. Her memories hung heavy in that laugh, a weighted sound that slammed into me and knocked the words from my mouth. I felt like a kid again, standing by her at the stove when she told me my mother should have been teaching me to cook, when she told me to stir the pot from the bottom or the slip dumplings would stick together, when she taught me to light a cigarette, when she slapped my back while I choked on *Jack Daniels*, when she took me to buy my first pack of tampons and told me again and again, "You ain't dyin', girl."

"We don't have no say, 'cause we was an afterthought. He yanked us up out o' man's ribs, but He made man out the Earth. He made him out the dirt and the mud and made him out the world, so man is the world. Women…women just a part o' men." Elaine snubbed the cigarette out, tapped the dark leather case on the edge of the table and I watched as another slim, white stick slid free. Within moments it was in the crease in her lips, that spot that over years of constant use had worn down and thinned and left Elaine with a face that only smiled halfway, that frowned all the time, and made her look like a fish out of water, gasping for breath, when the little stick appendage was missing from its place.

"I think you're living in the past. We've done all kinds of things. We're important now, and they know it. This isn't some…third world country. It's America. You know? Like, you're free to say this. No man is stopping you." Elaine grabbed the water-beaded bag of peas and shoved it back against my face, so that I had to grab it and hold it in place. "You goin' to have yourself a pretty little mark there," she said, as if she were content to just change the topic.

"Badge of honor," I smiled, proud of myself. "I said what I needed to say. I stood up for myself."

"Bag o' peas," she said. "What a woman got, huh? Bag o' peas and heretic. "

"Heroine," I countered.

"Heredity. History. It's the same thing." Elaine stood and made her way to the pot on the stove, turning it on so the water would begin to boil. "Hand me those peas. They ain't helpin' you no ways."

Be Proud

I am fully capable of bringing a man
trembling to his knees.
I have seen myself do it,
once, twice, three times.
You fell down begging for my heart
and a place for the chain around my finger.
I don't plan, I plot.
I understand the layout, the scheme
long before you could realize
that with a silly, little bit of metal
you'd finally given me the power over you.
I am a professional mover,
a packer, a loader, a throw-it-in-a-boxer.
While you're away at work
I'm loading a truck with everything that isn't nailed
down.
I'm telling you, "I love you"
and asking what you want for dinner.
I'm fully capable of walking
in and out
of your life, in spiky high heeled shoes.
A bit of leg here, a bare shoulder there
and I can see you on your knees again,
begging for a place inside me.
I have spilled out life into the waiting hands.
I have cried in shame and pain and hate.
I have let loose my life blood:
murder at the end of every month.
I have earned the map of marks that mar

my belly, my breasts, my thighs.
I have loved and lost and given up.
I have said "Yes" and "I do".
I have filed complaints and decrees,
and signed my name in illegible script
across any number of legal documents.
And I have opened my thighs
and let you place your heart back between them:
soft against a place hard enough
to spit out life and snub you out,
like the fiery end of my menthol cigarette.
I have become everything you wanted,
the creature you molded.
I am fully capable of telling the tale,
my constant clumsy stories.
"I tripped and ran into his fist."
"I fell down the stairs of his knuckles."
"I slipped along the rough callous of his palm."
You molded me and made me.
Be proud.
I am fully capable of bringing you to your knees,
and you allow me to do it.

Aflame

They marched her in at gun point and like a moth
circling the flame, she did an elegant kamikaze dive into
it, her papery wings alighting in a blaze that fizzled out
with a shotgun blast bang. How many lives does one
little moth have?

Her mother found the worm of one inside the lid of
the children's Motrin bottle. It had cocooned itself in
thin, white threads and she set it on the counter, dumped
the thick liquid down the drain, and wondered if moths
got headaches or fevers.

So, she held the hollow tip against her child's back
and said, "Daughter, it is well." She directed her to the
right door, the right chair, and gave her the right
magazine. *Garbage in, garbage out.* She rolled the slick
paper tight and slapped it down on the head of a fly, a
moth, something with wings. Then, ripping free one
page at a time, she handed them to her daughter, who
crumpled them up and shoved them in her mouth. She
chewed and swallowed.

Now this daughter turns the porch light on and off.
She listens to the tap, tap, tap of the little wings, the tiny
bodies, as they slam, slam, slam against the glass. On
and off. On and off. Tap, tap, tap.

For Her

So she's sitting there
in her lacy bra and panty set
that has to match
no matter the occasion
or whether she believes
there's some chance she's
getting laid. Amazingly enough,
she's got less up top
than her aging boss
who could use a bra of his
own to hold in his
jiggly bits. And thank
God for the "for her" car
in its rosy pink color.
We wouldn't want the men
to have to guess at
the driving skill of their
fellow daily, dim, dense
traffic jam partners.
And she'll go home tonight
to her razor/vibrator combo
pack and plan a night of
living on the edge. After
a long day at the office
where the men all finally
paid attention (thanks surely
to her butt enhancing
panties), she's ready for a

little one on one on one
with her pink little machine
and her double A batteries.
So it's little surprise that
she can handle when she gets home
and fires up a recipe for fun,
that the batteries buzz, buzz, buzz
right to death. Phillips head
screwdriver. She's searching her
little pink tool box, because
any other shade hurts her eyes,
and it's the only one that comes
with the cute little labels
in the shape of hearts
that tell her the names of these
cavemanesque tools.
By the time she's done
and she's found her tool
and replaced the batteries
and is ready to roll and rock,
she rolls herself right into
bed and rocks herself to sleep.
Taking only a few moments
to scrawl it all down, her little
pink life in her voice activated,
password protected Lisa Frank
journal . And she's writing this all
with her Bic For Her pen.

Deuteronomy 25:11-12

[11] *If two men are fighting and the wife of one of them comes to rescue*

her husband from his assailant, and she reaches out and seizes him

by his private parts, [12] *you shall cut off her hand. Show her no pity.*

It's like watching a dance,
the combined moves
of fists and knees.
The smack and thud
and bang and bash
and crunch of knuckles
on a bare, pale cheek.
They're beating him
to consciousness,
for herself at least,
who knows
Tae Kwon Kick-Your-Ass.
And she's in the middle
of the dance dance revolution.
Reaching out a hand to force
a pirouette on his frenemy's
cash and prizes
his Cracker Jacks,
his love spuds,
his secrets.
And it's slam
bang
bash

back into the not-getting-any-younger
witness. The getting on
tribute. And she saved what
was left of his life,
sacrificing dignity and pride
for the sake of fourteen bones
in the making of a smile
or wink.
She's a discount shopper
who got scammed by the clause
of the tiny print at the bottom
that for every fourteen saved
one loses 27.

E!strogen Tonight

Scene begins in a crowded newsroom. Cameras everywhere. Main desk is seated right in the middle with Holly and Candice sitting behind it, ready to begin after the short commercial break. Weather station is off to the side, where Leeann waits.

Holly: *(Sitting behind newsdesk, smiling, friendly. Shuffling papers in her hands before looking up at the camera.)* Tonight, a man speaks out against the new law passed in Congress today. President Gilman has certainly created a stir with this bold move, yet still sees a rise in support from women voters.

Candice: *(Sitting beside Holly. Smiles to the camera and motions off screen towards Leeann.)* More on that later. Now, let's turn it over to Leeann with the weather. I know we're all very concerned with the impact of this newest hurricane. Leeann?

Leeann: *(Standing before a large weather screen and motioning towards Florida and the Eastern seaboard.)* Thank you Candice. Hurricane Brett is still sweeping across the Eastern seaboard, leaving behind wreckage and a rising death toll, the likes of which haven't been seen in over 128 years, back when Hurricane Catrina devastated New Orleans. Women are being instructed to keep their families, pets and other belongings inside...

Scene fades from the newsroom to a small rural development. A news van is parked by the sidewalk, where Andrea is preparing for her interview with Mr. Thomas. Mariel adjusts the camera equipment.

Andrea: *(Standing by the van door, checking reflection in the side mirror, while Mr. Thomas paces along the sidewalk. Turns and notices him.)* You going to be able to handle this?

Mr. Thomas: *(Obviously nervous, wiping hands on pants. Holding them then behind his back and straightening his shoulders.)* Yeah. I mean...yes, Ma'am.

Mariel: *(Appears with camera.)* Two minutes.

Andrea: *(Steps up next to Mr. Thomas, holding a microphone.)* Okay, Mr. Thomas. Smile. Speak clearly. Take your time. You've only got a few moments, so make them count. You're preaching to a crowd that's not likely to want to hear what you have to say. I'll try to help as much as I can.

Mr. Thomas: Thank you, Ma'am.

Holly: *(Voice cues in for Andrea)* And now to Andrea, who's in Belview. How are the people reacting to the news today from Congress, Andrea?

Andrea: *(Holds the mic to her mouth, smiles brightly and speaks to the camera.)* Thank you, Holly. The emotions are certainly mixed throughout the country after Congress announced the landslide that saw No Right to Choose put through into law. I'm here with Mr. Thomas, a local homeowner who runs a small internet company from his home. *(Turning to Mr. Thomas.)* Mr. Thomas, can you tell me your feelings on this bold move by President Gilman? How are you, and men like yourself, reacting to the news?

Mr. Thomas: *(Looks nervous as Andrea puts the microphone to his face. Stutters.)* Well...like I know a long time ago men tried to do this, this kinda...stuff...to women...

Andrea: *(Interrupts)* What kind of stuff was that, Mr. Thomas?

Mr. Thomas: *(Slightly flustered by her making him say it.)* Oh you know. Like having babies and stuff.

Andrea: I see.

Mr. Thomas: But we saw it wasn't right, you know? It didn't work. So now...well...making it so a man doesn't have a choice, well that just don't seem right.

Andrea: And why is that?

Mr. Thomas: *(Grows increasingly flustered)* Well what if they look at me and say 'You don't make enough money to have more kids.' Then I have to go have a...you know...

Andrea: A vasectomy.

Mr. Thomas: *(Extremely uncomfortable with that word.)* Yeah. That. Who the hell has the right to tell me if I can have kids? Or make me have surgery!

Andrea: You realize, Mr. Thomas, that the procedure is reversible if the man can later prove to be more financially stable. The idea is to help ease the burden of the government systems by making sure that men are financially capable of rearing a child.

Mr. Thomas: Well yeah, but...but like I have to have another surgery then if they say it's okay? Or...or what if they see I have two kids by different mothers? Or I got married too many times! I didn't, but what if, you know? Or I...you know...I got something.

Andrea: Or if you'd contracted a disease?

Mr. Thomas: *(Definitely more upset.)* Now look. I don't have any junk like that, but, it's the principle of it. They'd make me...you know.

Andrea: Remove your penis?

Mr. Thomas: *(Shock. Outrage. Fear)* YEAH! That's mine! I don't want no one to take it!

Andrea: Do you realize, Mr. Thomas, that they have now proven men who sleep around are more likely to father children that end up using state programs for care when the father inevitably exits the picture? Are you also aware that that kind of promiscuity is the leading cause of disease that can be passed on to numerous partners? Or that the burden of care lays on the woman for a man's choice to act in such a promiscuous manner?

Mr. Thomas: *(Abashed. Confused.)* Well, I don't know about all that.

Andrea: *(Continues, no longer interviewing but interrogating him.)* That's right. You don't know about all that.

Mr. Thomas: Just don't think they have a right to tell us what to do with our bodies. Even...even if the Goddess says it ain't right.

Andrea: *(Smart-assed. Flippant. Condescending.)* This isn't 2012 anymore, Mr. Thomas. That ridiculous attitude of separation of Church and State was fundamentally wrong. This country was founded under the gospels of the Goddess, and it is by those standards that this law was passed.

Mr. Thomas: I'm sure you're right, Ma'am. God...Goddess bless you, Ma'am. I should be going now.

Andrea: *(Turns back to the camera as Mr. Thomas walks up the sidewalk and into his house.)* Thank you, Mr. Thomas. Holly, this seems to be the general feeling among men in the aftermath of such a promising move forward. It will take time, but we can be assured that understanding and general acceptance is well on its way. Back to you in the studio.

Holly: Thank you Andrea. Now on to sports. Women's Basketball star...

Melody

My hips are playing sweet melodies
of the snap, crackle, and pop.
It's got to be from all those years
of the on my knees,
legs bent,
back arched,
shoving out of life.
Yes, the tune I sing
is one of midnight fevers
and shit I have to pee again.
I'm tracing the lines of
the pathways marked across my skin,
in bluish white tint
like crooked veins
saying, "Hey, I was here".
As if I'd forget,
they had to leave a lasting impression.
So the snap, crackle, pop
sounds like, "Mommy I love you".
It's bath water splashing
and terrifying temper tantrums.
It's a poke in the eye
that results in multiple trips
to the emergency room
and medication
to this day.
And my soul is a one-eyed crow
staring off in the wrong direction,
so I missed it.

I missed the song.
I sat back and watched the wrong way
and the melody seeped away.

I've Given Some Thought to Traveling

I'm fully aware that my first part of the journey cannot take me anywhere near Headland, Alaska. See, I'm conscious of the fact (though I've never boarded a plane in my life) that there is truly no comfortable way to travel except in one's nightgown. I would certainly prefer not to begin my journey with an impromptu crime spree. So sorry, Alaska, Palin, dog sleds, and the Deathly Dalton Highway.

I'm considering instead on beginning my trip in the sunny state of Florida. However, with my nice little private jet shooting me through the clouds, all in the comfort of my Victoria Secret nightgown, I have every intention on enjoying a bit of death-defying acts of terror/stupidity/false bravery and parachuting my way into the land of oranges, hurricanes, and the source of endless songs with barely clad women, beat box bass, and shining beaches. Unfortunately, I am divorced and since I only perform acts of courageousness on Sundays, when everyone else is resting, I'm afraid I simply wouldn't be allowed to. The plane would taxi in, drop me off nice as can be, and I'd never have a chance to sky-dive into the ample cleavage of a music video bikini model.

So I can't go up and I can't go down. I'm figuring I'll shoot for somewhere in the middle. I'll make it like a circle and work my way out, spiral around and around and hit all the spots. I'm eyeballing a map and my hazel orbs settle on Kentucky: the home of the derby, bluegrass museums and bourbon. I can't go wrong with a bit of bourbon, but I have a bad habit. After a drink or two, I end up down to my bikini, wandering the side of the highway. I only hope I manage to make friends with at least two officers to escort me on my road-walking mission. Otherwise, I suppose I'll have to invest in a club. If only I didn't fall between the 90 and 200 pound weight restrictions. Damn me and my relatively healthy lifestyle choices.

Fine, fine. I'm headed to Montana. There's not much to see besides the mountains, the wildlife, and one epic, angry geyser. Drinking is inevitable, and I've heard the salons are top notch. I've packed my custom Weight Watchers scale. I've chosen each of my outfits with care, so regardless of my penchant for off the cuff strip sessions, I'll be sure to always have on at least three pounds and two ounces of clothing. My dancing skills aren't great anyway, but everything improves from the height of a bar table.

This habit of mine for stripping down could really cause me trouble in Oxford, Ohio. I always carry a picture of my boyfriend with me. It sure would be hard to get undressed at night without his pixilated eyes seeing my nakedness.

You know what, I have a better thought. I'll simply head for Virginia. I hear the corset inspectors are top notch, and I really need to have mine checked out. I never can tell if they are fitting quite the way they are supposed to. I happen to love my corsets though, so the idea of traveling to a land where people recognize their beauty in such a way as to make it illegal not to wear one, well, sounds like home to me.

That being said, I'll have to avoid Merryville, Missouri. Unless that is I intend to leave the corsets behind. I wouldn't want to deny the men there the view of my unencumbered body; though Gods know the only curves I carry come out with the boning.

Hell, had I know that Illinois was a BDSM community at the beginning of my trip, I'd have begun and probably ended there. There's nothing so sweet as calling a man "Master". I wonder if they hand out collars at the airport. Perhaps I'll just pack my own.

Oh this is ridiculous. Here I am, twenty bags in and I'm so confused. My Bic For Her pen ran out of purple ink and I've forgotten if the brown bag contains the right ingredients for a lawful trip to Oakland or Jacksonville. The pink is certainly for Los Angeles, or was it Portland? You know what? I bet the falls in Niagara are beautiful this time of year. Now, to find my passport…

Without Emotions

Without emotions, our bodies become
one big, ticking clock. I'm
feeling my uterus twinkling away
like a second hand skipping on
a Little Boy bomb. Tick, tick,
tick.

And it's nuclear war on the highest,
smallest level. My own cells are
prisons for the soldiers of the
Tick Tock battle. A band
of twisters, turners, and traitors,
with the cruel intentions to
end life before the twinkle enters
the eye.

Jars and Capes and Broken Things

I'm a cause, like save the whales, or the Bengal tigers, or the Giant Panda. I'm lost and running around with my GPS turned upside down, and Tom-Tom keeps telling me to turn left in point one miles. Turn left in point one miles. I'm a cat in a tree. A lost puppy with reward posters up and I keep wondering how much I'm worth, but puppies can't read. So, I'm staring at a picture of myself, in little kid cartoon hands, with thick crayon swipes to show the emotion, the pain, the loss. I'm lost.

I'm surrounded by the spandex and cape types. They're either superheroes or professional wrestlers. Everyone wants to save a broken thing. They show up with their tool-belts and duct tape and they're ready to fix me. I'm one to be fixed. They want to mow my lawn for me and fix the leaky pipes. They want to take me shopping and fix my image. They want to open jars for me and stuff all my confusing, female emotions down into the bottom of them…cover them up with seedy jams and homemade spaghetti sauce.

They've all got an agenda and a superhero complex. I'm still searching for their kryptonite, the key to bringing them to their knees. I want that moment, where I'm feeling a little less lost and a lot more in control. Maybe the cat isn't stuck, but she just likes the view. I've always had a thing for heights. I'd look better in the spandex. I ought to have my own cape. I want to be every character in this story: the hero, the victim, the villain. I want to mow my own lawn and I'm gnawing away at the grass, shredding it with my teeth, to get to the down and dirty of it. I want to get into the earth, because that's where superheroes come from. And I want a cape, a red cape that shines in the light. And I want to open my own damn jars.

Here is a preview of the next book in

Laura A. Lord's

collection.

Perjury

Available Summer 2014

History of a Woman

She is Raging

Her every step has set the ground to
Shaking; quaking and trembling,
it's breaking off at the edges
and swallowing up every ounce
of the requiem, of grief.
The calling of sincerity.
The jeers slipping in her veins
and boiling, bubbling under the surface.
The pressure is building and steam
falls in droplets, carving canyons into
the pale framework of her cheeks.
The landscape has shifted,
rushing in. The scaffolding that held
her little world in place
has turned liquid and swept her
straight off her feet.
She's sucked up all her skeletons
in the whirlwind of her desire
and torrents of hopelessness have
blackened out the design.
It's opening inside her:
a daybreak that looks like twilight.
Her womb unlocks like a fissure and there
the storm rages on.
The thump, thump, thump
of her latest plummet.
She does not fall gracefully.
She crawls through the sludge
of her latest defeat, barely on her knees.

Her hands dip into the typhoon,
the endless well of emptiness.
She screams in silent pleas.
A storm bound and bent on the decline
of civilizations, of peoples, of hopes
She's hollowed out her place here.
She's settled into the void.
The unfilled.
The vacant.
Carnivorous yearning,
ravenous famine.
Her words are a pestilence,
a plague on those who have stepped back
to watch the rupture,
to mend the breach.
Storm chasers, paparazzi.
She is an epidemic,
Widespread, unchecked,
and unbridled.
Rampant and wild,
she is filling this world.
Encompassing.
Raging.

Laura A. Lord

Laura A. Lord is a graduate of Chesapeake College. She is the author of *Wake Up a Woman*, *History of a Woman*, and *The Telling*. Her work has been published in *The Beacon*, *Whirl with Words*, and *The Collegian*. She lives on the Eastern Shore of Maryland with her husband and her two children.

Please visit

Historyofawoman.com

Photographer: Linzi Marvel